T0199017

The First Christmas Tree

R.S. Batson

WestBow Press books may be ordered through booksellers or by contacting:

WestBow Press
A Division of Thomas Nelson & Zondervan
1663 Liberty Drive
Bloomington, IN 47403
www.westbowpress.com
844.714.3454

Because of the dynamic nature of the Internet, any web addresses or links contained in this book may have changed
since publication and may no longer be valid. The views expressed in this work are solely those of the author and do
not necessarily reflect the views of the publisher, and the publisher hereby disclaims any responsibility for them.

Any people depicted in stock imagery provided by Getty Images are models, and such images are being used for illustrative purposes only.
Certain stock imagery © Getty Images.

ISBN: 978-1-6642-0981-7 (sc)
ISBN: 978-1-6642-0983-1 (hc)
ISBN: 978-1-6642-0982-4 (e)

Library of Congress Control Number: 2020920727

Print information available on the last page.

WestBow Press rev. date: 11/04/2020

WESTBOW
PRESS®
A DIVISION OF THOMAS NELSON
& ZONDERVAN

By Gladys Nichols Norbit 1907-2002, as told by her
mother Katy Vaughan Nichols 1878-1957

Originally Recorded by Cathy Porter James, 2000 (Katy's Great Granddaughter)

Retold by R.S. Batson, 2020 (Katy's Great, Great Grandson)

The skies were dark with snow clouds that cold December day in 1887. But Katy's heart was warm and light as she followed her brothers down the mountain side. She had never been so excited in her whole life, for she was on her way to see her very *First Christmas Tree!* Pa had been down to town the week before and was told by some of the townspeople that they were planning a Christmas party for the local children. There would be festivities with a big Christmas Tree, as well as gifts for each child who attended.

In recent years, Pa had been feeling poorly, so the doctor told him to move to the mountains. He told Pa that the higher altitude might improve his health. When Katy was nearly 10, she remembered moving, and how ominous the big mountain had looked in the distance as they headed up to their new homesite.

Her parents worked hard on their mountain farm to provide for their children. Even though there was very little money for extras, Katy and her brothers always had plenty to eat and warm clothes to wear.

2

So on that cold Christmas Eve morning, Katy and her brothers woke up early and got dressed in their Sunday best, before sitting down for breakfast. Katy was too excited to eat, but her brothers reminded her that it was a 6 mile walk to town and she needed to have a good breakfast in her before they left for the Christmas Party.

As they walked down the road they were joined by Katy's friend Prissy and her brothers. All the way to town the little girls gushed about the magical time they would have at the Christmas Party. When they reached town at midday, Prissy's older sister welcomed them into her home and fed them a hearty lunch. They were grateful and eagerly ate every bite, for they were *very* hungry from their long walk.

6

After eating, even though it was a bit early, they walked over to the schoolhouse where the party was to be held. They were just too excited to do anything else! When they walked in, they saw people decorating a Christmas tree and wrapping gifts. Katy and Prissy sat quietly on the back seat, just so they could watch all the activity. They had never seen a spectacle quite like this and were too stunned to do or say much else! After a bit, a lovely lady strolled over to them. She told them that her name was Mrs. Miles and she was married to Doc Miles, the town's only doctor. Katy remembered him from when he had ridden up the mountain to set her brother's broken arm. Mrs. Miles asked them their names and if they were staying for the Christmas party. They both eagerly shook their heads yes! So she took down their names in a little black book and as she wrote, she asked the names of both Katy and Prissy's brothers. For a moment Katy wondered why Mrs. Miles would want to write all of their names down, but soon forgot all about it in the excitement. Finally the children went back to Prissy's sister's house to wait for the party to begin.

Later, when it was time to go back over to the schoolhouse, they were so excited, the children's feet barely touched the ground as they skipped along! When they walked in, Katy couldn't remember ever seeing anything quite so beautiful as the Christmas Tree. It was decorated with strings of colored popcorn, glass ornaments and glowed with lighted candles! It was absolutely spectacular!

The children thought the program was wonderful! There was carol singing, Christmas stories and cakes and candies to eat. Then, as the events started to die down, Doc Miles burst into the room and exclaimed, " We have a special surprise guest who just arrived"...then Santa Claus himself bounded into the room right from behind the doctor. He was carrying a big bag full of gifts on his back! He greeted the children with a hearty "HO,HO,HO"! Then he pulled out a strangely familiar black book from his big, red jacket and began to read the children's names written down on the pages.

As each name was called, Santa would reach down into his bag and pull out a gift. He would then hand it to one of the grown-ups to give to the child whose name had been read. As this continued for several minutes, Katy, Prissy and their brothers all watched wistfully. They were sure that their names would NOT be called because no one in town really knew them. Then at that moment, Santa read Prissy's name out loud! She was so surprised! Katy thought that perhaps Prissy's sister had somehow arranged it. She excitedly answered "Present!"...as all the other children had done. Then a nice lady took a small wrapped box from Santa and brought it over to her. She carefully removed the beautifully colored wrapping paper, and was delighted to find that she had received a lovely hair brush and comb set. Katy had been wishing for a brush and comb set just like that, but was still very glad for her little friend.

So as the time went by, Santa continued to call out children's names. But Katy knew that her real gift was just to get to attend the beautiful party with her friends. She sat beaming with Christmas Spirit watching the other children opening their gifts. Then suddenly, to her surprise, she heard Santa call out "Katy?!"...For a split second, she was too surprised to answer! Then somehow she managed to squeak weakly, "present?"...When her present was given to her she was so excited that she could hardly open it! When she finally got it open, she found a brush and comb set, just like Prissy's! She was so overcome with joy, she started to cry! After seeing her reaction, her brothers started to snicker and laugh...Then she heard hers and Prissy's brothers names called as well, as they all began to laugh and cry with joy! Katy figured that Doc's wife had acted as one of Santa's helpers by making sure all the children's names at the party had been written down in Santa's little black book. Not a single child would miss out on getting a Christmas gift from Santa!

That morning, before leaving home, Pa had given the children each ten cents. That was a pretty fair amount of money for back then, but Pa had gotten in a good harvest that year and had a little extra. He wanted to make sure his children had a special Christmas. It actually was the first money Katy ever had of her own to spend on anything she wanted. So before making that long walk home, the children stopped by the general store. The store owner was just about the lock up, but smiled and threw open the door for the kids. He was a very nice man, but Katy wondered about the big bag in the corner of the store. It looked just like the one Santa had, but the store owner assured her it was just a bag of old table cloths. Katy noticed that the table cloths appeared to be red. He just smiled at her as he picked it up and carried it to the back room of his store. Katy was so excited to get to buy something with her own money, she barely paid him any mind as he walked by her. Katy was truly perplexed! She had no idea what she should buy with her money. There were so many beautiful and interesting things in the store. Then her eyes fell on a little candy hen sitting on its very own little candy nest. The candy nest was made up into the shape of a tiny basket. When she picked the little hen up, she found that the basket was filled with jellybeans. That was it then. That was what she would buy. But her heart sank as she read the price tag. It was marked for 25 Cents. The store owner was watching her closely and saw the look on her face as she turned the hen over to read the tag. He smiled to himself as he walked over to her to ask her how much money she had to spend. She meekly held up her dime to show him...The store owner frowned and shook his head and said, "I'm sorry, but that hen cost 25 cents"...but then he burst out into a big grin and told her that it just so happened that the candy hen had a special Christmas sale price of 10 cents just for today! Katy was overjoyed!

After everyone was finished with their shopping, it was time to head home. Katy, Prissy and their brothers all said their goodbyes, and the children started the long walk up the mountain side. They had a six mile journey and their parents would start to worry if they weren't home soon. The clouds still hung low on the mountain and soon the snow began to fall. But Katy and her brothers could barely feel the cold. They were all glowing with a warm Christmas Spirit from within!

When they finally reached their home, Ma and Pa were anxiously watching for them. When they got inside the warm house they were greeted by the smell of a big dinner and a roaring fire. The children were all very hungry. As they sat down at the dinner table, the entire family held hands and bowed their heads. Pa thanked God for the many blessings that had been bestowed on his family, and for GOD keeping his children safe on their journey to town. Pa also thanked GOD for sending his SON, JESUS, to us and hoped everyone would remember why we celebrate the birth of HIS SON during this special time of year. As they all began to eat, the children told their parents of the wonderful time they all had. Ma and Pa felt so blessed that their children were able to experience such a special Christmas!

That night, as Katy lay in her bed, she could barely keep her eyes open, in spite of the excitement of the day. Just as she drifted off to sleep she pictured that beautiful, *First Christmas Tree* in her head, and thought she could hear Santa Claus exclaim, "Merry Christmas Katy, and to all a good night"...!

Author Biography

R.S. Batson is a born and raised Texan, who lives with his family in Fort Worth, Texas. While helping raise his 3 children (Ella 10, Emma 7 and Jake 3), he stays busy with his voice acting activities, while working on his next book.

Katy Vaughan Nichols
1878-1957

Katy was born in a log cabin that her father had built by himself in the foothills of NE Arkansas, around 1880. Although they were relatively poor, Katy grew up in a happy home. At a very young age, she learned from her mother how to sew and cook, as well as how to grow the food they needed to survive, from her father. She grew up in a family of faith and love. She eventually was known to be a wonderful story teller and would regale her children, grandchildren and great grandchildren about stories of trading goods with Indians, bushwhackers, highwaymen and Civil War soldiers. Katy also loved to tell ghost stories, delighting in scaring children and adults alike! With a twinkle in her eye and a sweet smile on her face, she lived a joyful happy life, in spite of going blind at a relatively young age. By most accounts, Katy was always happy and in a good mood, inspiring those who knew her, and future generations of her family to trust in their faith and each other, to see things through when life turned rough.

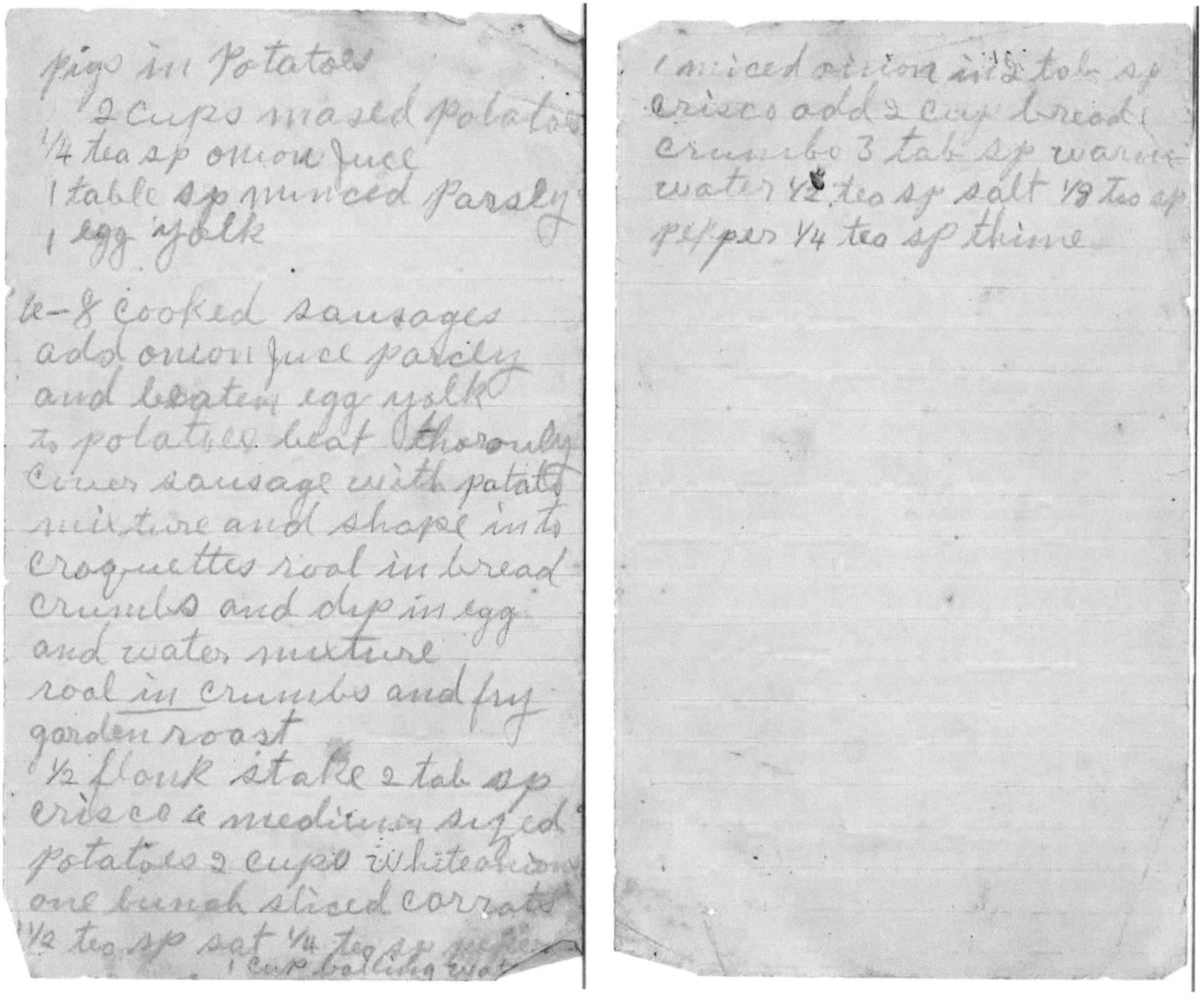

pigs in Potatoes
2 cups mashed potatoes
1/4 tea sp onion juce
1 table sp minced Parsley
1 egg yolk

6-8 cooked sausages
add onion juce parcly
and beaten egg yolk
to potatoes beat thoroughly
Cover sausage with potato
mixture and shape into
croquettes roal in bread
crumbs and dip in egg
and water mixture
roal in crumbs and fry

garden roast
1/2 flank stake 2 tab sp
crisco 4 medium sized
potatoes 2 cups white onion
one bunch sliced carrots
1/2 tea sp sat 1/4 tea sp pepper
1 cup boiling wat

1 minced onion in 2 tab sp
crisco add 2 cup bread
crumbs 3 tab sp warm
water 1/2 tea sp salt 1/8 tea sp
pepper 1/4 tea sp thime

Caned pimentos
or thick mealed peppers
cut tops off and remove
seeds from both red
and green peppers
sprinkle with salt
cover with boiling
water. let stand 2 or 3 hours
for eache cup of vinegar
add 1 cup of sugar
and boil to a syrup
drain peppers and put
in syrup cook until
tender & pack in hot
pint jars cover with
hot syrup

tamale loaf

⅓ cup red onion, chopped
2 ½ cups tomatoes
1 cup corn meal
2 cups ground meat
2 eggs 1 ½ teasp salt
1 teasp paprika
½ teasp pepper ¾ cup corn
fry onion in crisco
until lightly browned
add tomatoes when hot
stir in corn meal cook
10 minutes stir to
prevent lumping
remove from fire
add seasoning meat
corn corn and eggs
blend thoroughly
pour in pan bake 45
minutes

---

roman holiday

¼ cup crisco 1 onion chopped
2 cups cooked spaghetti
1 lb hamburger 1 teasp salt
½ teasp pepper 1 ½ cups
canned tomatoes ½ grated
cheese fry onions in
crisco add meat and
seasoning cook 5 minutes
make a layer of spaghetti
in a baking dish add
meat mixture and
drippings then another
layer of spaghetti pour
in tomatoes sprinkle
grated cheese cover dish
bake in moderate oven

Pigs in Potatoes

2 cups of mashed potatoes
¼ tsp of onion juice
1 Tbsp. of minced parsley
1 egg yolk
6 to 8 cooked sausages

Add onion juice, parsley and egg yolk to mashed potatoes. Beat thoroughly. Cover sausage with potato mix and shape into croquettes, roll in bread crumbs and dip in egg and water mixture. Roll in crumbs and fry.

Garden Roast

½ flank steak
2 tbsp. Crisco
2 cups white onions
1 bunch sliced carrots
½ tsp salt
¼ tsp pepper
1 cup boiling water

No further instructions were given for this recipe but I would assume she cooked on the stove until done.

Typed translation of handwritten recipes

Canned Pimentos (or thick mealed peppers)

Cut tops off peppers and remove seeds from both red and green peppers. Sprinkle with salt and cover with boiling water. Let stand 2 to 3 hours. Add one cup to of sugar to each cup of vinegar and boil to a syrup. Drain peppers and put in syrup. Cook until tender. Pack in hot pint jars and cover with hot syrup.

Tamale Loaf

1/3 cup Crisco
2 ½ cups chopped tomatoes
1 cup corn meal
2 cups ground meat
2 eggs
1 ½ tsp salt
1 tsp paprika
¾ cup corn

Fry onions in Crisco until lightly browned. Add tomatoes. When hot stir in corn meal. Cook 10 minutes. Stir to prevent lumping. Remove from fire. Add seasoned meat, can corn and eggs. Blend thoroughly, pour into pan and bake 45 minutes.

Typed translation of handwritten recipes

27

Roman Holiday

¼ cup Crisco
1 onion chopped
2 cups cooked spaghetti
1 lb. hamburger meat
1 tsp salt
1 ½ cup canned tomatoes
¾ cup grated cheese

Fry onions in Crisco. Add meat and seasoning and cook 5 minutes. Make a layer of spaghetti in baking dish. Add meat mixture and drippings. Then add another layer of spaghetti. Pour in tomatoes and sprinkle cheese. Cover dish. Bake in moderate oven.

Typed translation of handwritten recipes

Emma Cate Batson 7 yrs old (Katy's Great-Great-Great Granddaughter)

29

Ella Batson 10 yrs old (Katy's Great-Great-Great Granddaughter)

Printed in the United States
By Bookmasters